© 2019 Azure Forte

Fielding Anger

All rights reserved. No part of this publication may be reproduced, stored in a retrieval system or transmited in any form or by any means, electronic, mechanical, photocopying, recording or otherwise without the prior permission of the publisher or in accordance with the provisions of the Copyright, Designs and Patents Act 1988 or under the terms of any licence permitting limited copying issued by the Copyright Licensing Angency.

ISBN-13: 978 0 69217 864 5

Azure Forte
FIELDING ANGER

Fielding Anger

AZURE FORTE

For Everyone

Contents

Introduction 1
Guidelines 3
Guidelines 4
Who Should Use This Guide 5
How to Use This Book 6
The Most Important Things to Know 9
Toolbox 19
What Causes Anger? 20
Putting Brainpower Up Front 23
Letting Logic Have a Say 28
Fact and Feeling Team Work 30
Six Step Anger Event Worksheet 34
The Double-down Dilemma 44
Exploring the Underground 47
The Self Acceptance
Underground 50
Changing Blame to Regret 52
Realizing Inclusion 55
Dealing With A Bully 65
Knowing the Bully's Moves 66
The Mistake I Don't Want to Make 70
Avoiding a Trap 72
Exploring All Options 77
Avoiding the
Land of the Lost 79
The Move that Works 95
The Land of the Future 99
21st Century Anger 100
How to Learn a New Skill 107
21st Century Skills 108
12 Tips for Resolving a Conflict With
Another Person 111

"Who Shall Survive?" 113
Sociometry 114
Reader's Guide 115
Tool Reference Guide 122
Discussion Group Guidelines 124
Acknowledgments 127
Afterward 128

Success Stories

People Who Made Me Angry Can't Do That Anymore 18
Prepared In Advance 21
Fact and Feeling 32
I Used The Worksheet 42
A Double Down Wake Up 48
Inclusion I Didn't Want 60
Inclusion I Wanted 62
I Learned His Moves and I Won 68
My Boss Was A Bully 74
HELP! HELP? 85
Going It Alone Is Not The Answer 96
I Chose The Future 102

AZURE FORTE

A field guide is
a tool used to
study nature.

Angry feelings are
a part of nature.

BOOK AUTHOR

"Fielding" is a word from sports. An athlete on the playing field makes decisions on what to do with the ball.

Decisions on what to do with anger are the same.

Definition of Fielding:

1. CATCH, stop, retrieve; return, throw back.

2. DEPLOY, position, range, dispose.

3. DEAL WITH, handle, cope with, answer, reply to, respond to.

This tool guide will

- Give new ways to succeed when anger happens.

- Help you find the way that works best for you.

This guide will not give quick solutions.

All angry situations require careful thought.

Who should use it?

Anyone who would like successful results from angry feelings. Anyone who would like shorter encounters with aggressive angry people.

How to Use This Book

1. **Read the next eight pages, "The Most Important Things to Know."**

    This section gives the information you need before you can make any of the other tools and exercises work. Read these pages carefully and go back to them every now and then.

2. **Open the Toolbox and choose the tools that you need.**

    No matter how complicated the conflict of anger gets, it all boils down to a basic structure. The toolbox pages give tips and exercises with practical everyday wording. Drawings of characters named "Blue Shirt" and "Green Shirt" demonstrate the tools. It's up to you to decide if you will flip through the different exercises, or to follow them in order of the page numbers. Your personal method is the one that will work best.

3. **Success.**

    The Toolbox includes success stories to help learn the use of the tools. The stories are real. Names and minor details have been changed and the authors' identities have been kept confidential.

    These are stories of people who have used anger well with careful thought. They want to grow the number of people in the world who will do the same. Think of them as your team support. Stories have titles and are printed in italics.

4. **Exactly How Do Tools Get Used?**

   The Reader's Guide gives a walkthrough description of how skills were used, or not needed, in the final story, "I Chose the Future."

5. **Don't be alone.**

   Talk with a friend or counselor who also reads this book.

6. **Build your personal guide.**

   Use your own thinking power to decide what will help and what won't. Add your own ideas and subtract the ones that don't work.

AZURE FORTE

The Most Important Things to Know

Angry feelings can make a person want to be aggressive.

Aggression creates counter aggression and more anger.

Many people don't realize when they are being aggressive.

Anger can be good. Think of anger as a success engine.

A lot of anger is a lot of energy.

Use it well and your life will improve.

Anger is a personal feeling.

Even if another person started the problem your angry feeling lives inside and your solution must begin inside yourself.

Blaming.

It might seem like blaming another person is fair, but blaming won't bring success.

The blamed person will feel defensive and fight back.

What is aggression?

Aggression is a verbal, physical or indirect attack:

Finger-pointing

Blaming

Striking at a target.

Blaming Myself

Blaming myself doesn't work either. It makes me feel like I'm not allowed to be human and make mistakes.

There are 4 types of aggression.

1. Explosive: Impulsive physical or verbal abuse.

2. Passive: Attempts to harm another without the person realizing what's happening.

3. Strategic: Carefully planned harmful behavior (the opposite of impulsive).

4. Quiet/Hidden: Being angry and convincing yourself that you are not angry. The hidden anger can jump out as aggression when least expected.

What Doesn't Work:

Trying to stop a bully doesn't work.

What Works:

Stopping the cycle of aggression works.

All the pages of this book offer tips and tools.

AZURE FORTE

SUCCESS STORY

People Who Made Me Angry Can't Do That Anymore

I saw the pages of this toolbox for what they are, a set of tools. It wasn't like when I bought a flat screen TV and all I had to do was follow the installation guide.

I knew that I had to be the one to imagine the outcome of my actions and choose each step along the way thoughtfully.

So I made a deal with my best friend: We each kept a copy so we could talk and call each other when feeling stuck or confused. We compared notes and shared stories.

Some of the tools worked really well. If I tried one that didn't meet the need at hand I went back to looking through the tools until I found something else. Sometimes I combined two or more tools together, leaving out some parts and adding my own personal touch.

All in all I'm enjoying my success. People who once were able to make me angry can't do that anymore.

Toolbox

A toolbox is a collection of things that get used to create something. The tools in this next section work the same way.

Try them out and practice using them. Allow mistakes and you will become skillful.

With careful thought you will have Power Tools.

What Causes Anger?

A List of Triggers

Look through the check list below and mark off those events that make you angry. The list is also useful to gain understanding of other people's anger.

- _ Insult
- _ Feeling attacked
- _ Not safe
- _ Feeling protective of self or loved ones
- _ Feeling repressed (pushed down or road blocked)
- _ Betrayal
- _ Not being included
- _ Being tricked
- _ Being lied to
- _ Being treated with indifference
- _ Violation of privacy and/or private space
- _ Extreme irritation
- _ Confusion
- _ Feeling judged
- _ The "tantrum" syndrome: anger when you can't have it your way.
- _ Being extremely tired
- _ Other:

SUCCESS STORY

Prepared In Advance

I easily understood my feelings of anger, but I had never taken the time to see how I get angry.

I read the causes of anger on this list and thought about each one.

I checked off three of them.

Aside from understanding myself better, I've been able to be prepared in advance for the possible trap into conflict. In other words, before I just jump into things I think about what's going to be happening and how I might feel. That allows me to be careful or even to just avoid getting involved.

Putting Brainpower Up Front

The brain's logic can be like the engine on a train moving life forward on track.

Angry feelings show up like a hijack, jumping into the engine and pushing logic out.

When impulsive dramatic thoughts take over, life becomes a runaway train heading for a crash.

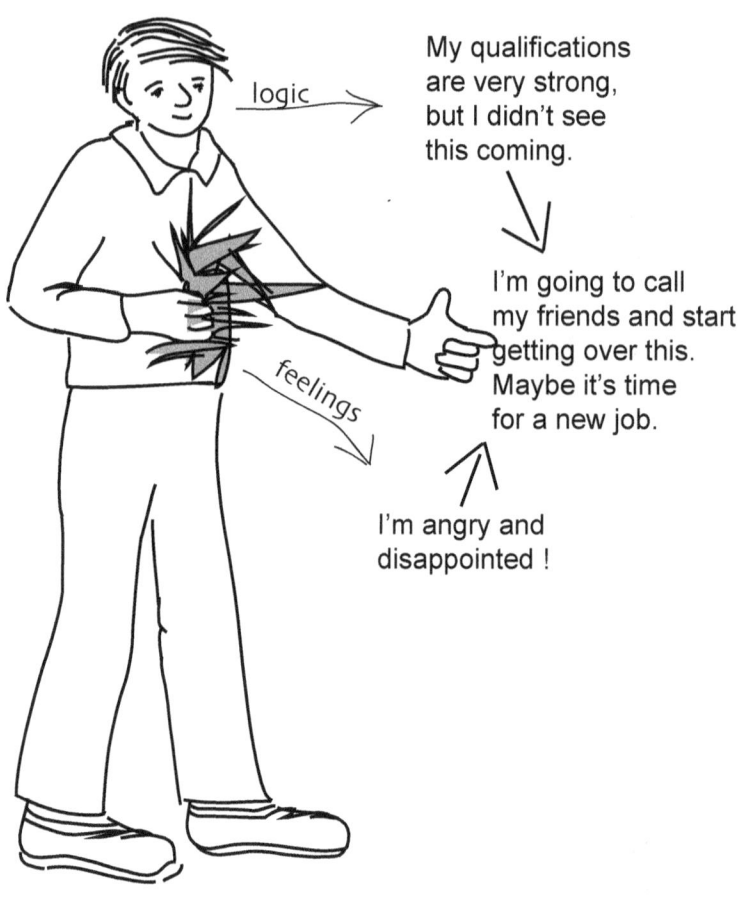

The skill of using full brain power relies on bringing logic back in. Feelings and logic work together to find a solution.

Five Steps to Prevent Feelings from Taking Control

1. Anger shows up.

2. Angry feelings start telling me what to do.

3. I make myself stop, wait and breathe.

4. I don't try to make my feelings go away.

5. I figure out a way to let logic back into my head.

Letting Logic Have a Say

Use this exercise to gain impulse control

(For one problem at a time).

1. Name a problem that made you angry.

2. Write the first thoughts that came to express your angry feelings.

3.   Now try to let logic back into the picture and write down the real facts.

4.   Compare the difference between feelings and facts.

Feelings	Facts

Fact and Feeling Team Work

Feelings alone aren't enough. Logic without feelings doesn't work either. Good ideas get started when feelings and logical thoughts listen to each other.

Working with a decision you are trying to make, or a problem you are having, use the cartoon to write down your feelings. Then search for facts and write them down. Imagine that your feelings and facts are talking to each other. Think about what's being said.

See if you can get an idea from this conversation.

FIELDING ANGER

Facts

Feelings

SUCCESS STORY

Fact and Feeling

I was known to all who care about me as "quick to explode." This wasn't exactly compatible with my wife's desire for peace and tranquility. When the arguments increased we got involved in marriage therapy. The process led us each to working on ourselves as individuals as well as married partners.

Learning new skills and building self-trust seemed to take a long time. At the peak of doubt that our marriage could be saved we were due to go on a family vacation with our kids. My teaching schedule and our kids' school vacations coincided, allowing a plan for me to go ahead with the kids two days early. Then my wife would join us at the end of her workweek.

Even with a vacation planned it wasn't a happy time. We were arguing and my short fuse was getting set whenever I felt criticized. My loss of endurance was overwhelming and I was convinced that getting divorced was the righteous next step. With an air of confidence, akin to laying down a royal flush in poker, I made the big D announcement, complete with planning options for selling the house and organizing parenting responsibilities. My wife was left to figure out whether she should skip the week of vacation, a la planning for divorce, or show up.

The kids and I arrived to the cottage. Within about 12 hours I was missing my wife, not even slightly ready to give up our marriage. I started making phone calls to convince her to join us.

I remember how pumped up I was with feeling when I made the divorce decision. It was as though I was made of feelings and nothing else, no logic, no careful thought. My feelings made me completely convinced that divorce was the right solution. Once that tidal wave of feeling ran its course my ability to think with logic returned. Fortunately my wife wasn't ready to give up either and we managed to have a decent vacation.

With practice I've been able to slow down when a feeling hijack sets in. It isn't easy. I can feel myself being driven with a looming promise that an impulsive act will make me feel better. Why doesn't human nature automatically give me a signal of how I will feel after the impulsive act?

I've learned a strategy of including a time cushion before I act on impulse. It's deliberate. At first it was unnatural. The more I've practiced the strategy, however, the more a feeling of habit has set in. At the precise moment that I want to leap with emotion it's becoming natural to wait instead.

Waiting gives me the advantage to include everything my thinking is made up of: feelings, logic, experience and wisdom.

Six Step Anger Event Worksheet

Each step of this exercise is like a clue in a detective story. The investigation will help solve the angry feelings.

First Step: Incident Report

Describe the Incident.
Make a brief report of what happened.
Leave out the details.

_____

_____

_____

_____

Identify the person, or persons, who made you angry. It's OK to name something abstract like Life or Bad Luck.

_____

_____

_____

_____

Second Step: Measurement

Measure the anger you have towards

whomever, or whatever, made you angry.

```
0 ----------------------------------------------- 10
Not Angry                                      Furious
```

Third Step: Intermission

You have created a statement of what happened and who should, or could, be held accountable.

A break is necessary before continuing to the forth step.

Do something relaxing.

<u>Fourth Step:</u> Search for Hidden Truth

To begin this step you must be comfortable, not hungry or tired.

The feelings towards the person who made you angry are obvious. You probably have non-obvious feelings that are hiding out. Look through this list as though you are studying a feeling X-ray.

Search for any of these feelings:

I am unhappy with myself.

I should have . . . . . .

I'm angry and I blame myself.

I wish I were a different type of person.

I don't trust myself.

I'm not good at relationships.

I'm not good at this exercise.

This Check List helps explore feelings of self-acceptance. Check the ones that are true for you.

- I have confidence and willingness to be Human and make mistakes.

- I feel a sense of belonging, even if other people are rejecting.

- Most of the time I listen to another person without having hopes of what the other will say.

- I either settle an argument without being aggressive or I retreat from the conflict.

- I use the fuel of anger to be proactive (I start to explore new constructive possibilities).

5th Step: Measure

Measure any feelings for yourself that are judgmental or blaming.

0 -- 10

Not beating up on myself   Can't stop being mad at me

Sixth Step: The Next Step

There are two jobs in the next step.

1. Clear up my feelings about myself.

2. If it's possible . . . straighten things out with the other person.

Many people want to know how to stop blaming or feeling bad about themselves.

There is no standard method. Each person finds their own solution.

Success is often gained by simply deciding, "I'm not going to beat up on myself."

Before I hold the other person accountable, I have to be OK with me.

SUCCESS STORY

I Used The Worksheet

With my daughter relocated across the country and a grandchild on the way it was time to regain some familiarity with air travel. It had been ten years since I'd flown anywhere.

I purchased a round-trip ticket and began to hyper-focus on preparing for the trip. I calculated how many pockets I needed in my travel clothing to store my ID, gate pass and cash for incidentals.

My list of Anger Triggers was well formulated. Too bad I didn't know about them.

Looking back I can clearly see it all:

- not feeling safe (fear of flying)
- feeling repressed (no time to do all the planned preparation)
- confusion (not knowing how things would be different since my last plane trip 10 years ago)
- Being extremely tired (I'd be less tired if I wasn't hyper-focused but I couldn't turn it off).

While I thought I was covering all bases for a smooth trip, I was unknowingly setting myself up for a meltdown. And here's how it almost happened.

The day before my trip I got myself packed and had only one task left, to shop for the perfect pair of travel cargo pants. I would not be rummaging around at the security gate, dropping things while groping through my purse. Not me. I would have it all under control.

I mapped out my shopping strategy perfectly. First a trip to the gym for my regular workout. (No point in boarding a plane for a 6 hour trip feeling like a lump.) Then to the shopping plaza.

I pulled up to the gym one hour before closing. "Hmmm, not very many cars in the parking lot. That's funny. Oh well." I grab my gear and head on in, only to be met at the door by the custodian.

His explanation: "The gym closes at 5 on Sundays" My response: "I thought the gym closed at 6!" His response: "No, it's always been 5 p.m."

Here's what I wanted to say (in rant tone), "Don't you people realize that some of us have to work all week!! The only time we get to go to the gym is on the weekends!! You really ought to show some consideration! The weekend isn't even half over!!"

Aside from the fact that the weekend was more than half over (it just felt like it wasn't), I miraculously didn't yell at the custodian. Maybe it was his evident appearance of wishing he was doing anything but sweeping a gym lobby at 5 p.m. on a Sunday. Or maybe it was some inborn understanding of how cruel I would be to yell at someone who had nothing to do with setting the gym hours. I pressed back to my car in what felt like an uphill climb, all the while wondering why I wanted to yell at someone who was not to blame. This was new for me.

I sat in the car unable to calm down. Finally I decided to try the Six-Step Anger Event Work Sheet. It took all six steps before I got in touch with my part in the mix up. 'Duh!' Whose job was it to be familiarized with the gym hours? I had been relying on a vague recollection of the schedule and had not bothered to look it up. I realized that my mistake was the major cause for missing my work out. I was relieved that I didn't yell at the custodian and was able to cut myself some slack. I knew I was having pre-travel jitters.

I'd be lying if I made this the end of the story. The real end of the story comes with my west coast arrival, de-boarding the plane and stepping up to the car rental counter. One quick efficient sweep into my cargo pants pocket for my driver's license, and presto: no license. It seems that the slant of the passenger seat (coach section) was the perfect angle for the license to slide out and slip away. But that's not the end of the story either.

The real end of the story isn't that I get a champion medal for planning. I get a gold medal for never beating up on myself, for being human. Eventually I managed to laugh at the whole thing. It was, after all, almost something I could sell to a stand up comedian.

A few weeks later my driver's license arrived via US Postal Service; return address Delta Airlines.

The Double-down Dilemma

In the picture on the right Blue Shirt and Green Shirt have missed the step of searching for deep-down feelings. They don't realize they are only half angry with each other.

The other half is the anger towards self. The hidden anger towards self sneaks in and doubles the anger towards the other person.

> Hidden feelings are a part of being human. It is also human to repair painful hidden feelings.

Exploring the Underground

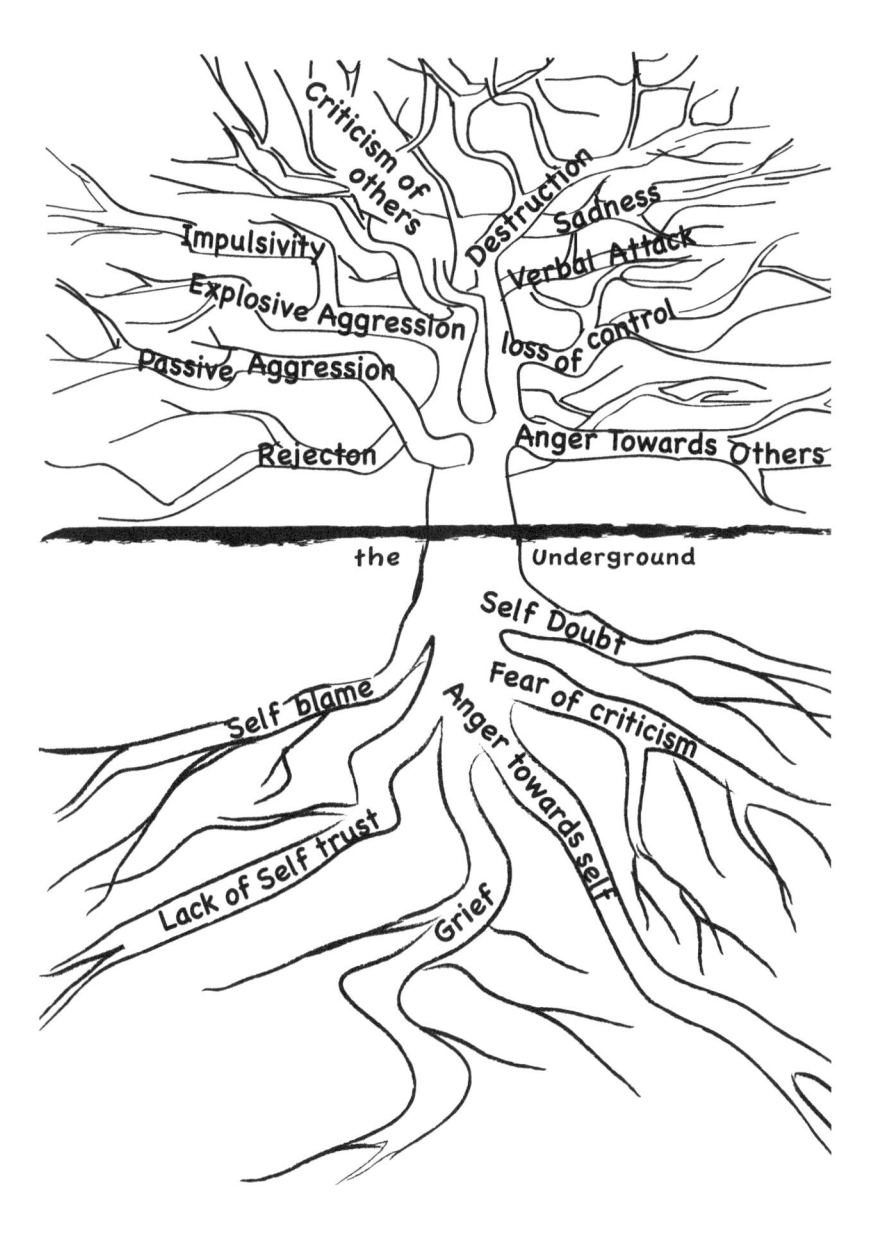

Tree diagram with branches labeled: Criticism of others, Impulsivity, Destruction, Sadness, Explosive Aggression, Verbal Attack, loss of control, Passive Aggression, Rejecton, Anger Towards Others. Below "the Underground" line, roots labeled: Self Doubt, Self blame, Fear of criticism, Lack of Self trust, Anger towards self, Grief.

This picture is an example of how hidden negative feelings can affect a person's life.

SUCCESS STORY

<u>A Double Down Wake Up</u>

I saw that I was accepting criticism on a regular basis from my significant other, Stan. Criticisms about others were also directed at me. He had an edge to him, always irritated and often sharp spoken. The turning point was about a coffee cup, "You're always leaving your coffee cup around the house. If you're not going to drink your coffee you should bring it to the sink, not just leave it there for me to see when I'm trying to relax."

At the time I did not understand why a simple thing like a coffee cup would prompt Stan to speak to me with an attacking tone. Nevertheless I actually accepted the idea that I had a deficiency and I didn't want to be deficient. I started making excuses, "I like to take my coffee with me when I'm going about the house. I don't really realize when I'm forgetting to pick it up."

I was getting defensive and again it wasn't working. I was angry at Stan for being picky and nasty.

So here's how the sequence went:

1. *Stan was feeling bad inside himself.*

2. *Stan, without realizing it, was throwing his discontent at me.*

3. *I thought I wanted to convince Stan to see me differently but in the deep down I wanted to feel OK about myself.*

4. *When Stan wouldn't change his opinion I got angry. My bad feeling about me made me want to throw the bad feeling back at him.*

Stan and I were each caught up in the Double Down Dilemma. In the moment of conflict Stan didn't like himself and he didn't like me. I didn't like me and I didn't like Stan.

This time I was sick of arguing. So instead of getting defensive I just took some time to think about it. I realized that my coffee cup misplacements weren't crimes. I had nothing to defend, other than being human.

This story isn't really about me and Stan. It's about me and me. From that day on I quit getting defensive. I don't mind being asked in a respectful way to make a change. But I don't accept attacking, blaming remarks.

If I'm going to negotiate with someone I do so from a place of self-acceptance. If I feel a little weak in the knees I take a strong stand of self-acceptance anyway, and the confident feeling shows up.

Stan and I didn't really last. I met someone new. One day, out of the blue, I was criticized for the way I react when watching a baseball game, "Your loud comments are very unattractive."

My response, "The way I watch baseball is one of the things I like about me."

We got to talk this one out in a civil fashion. Needless to say my friend decided to get involved in watching baseball games and gained great pleasure in following a major league team. The criticism of me seemed to disappear. We never did have to straighten it out.

The Self Acceptance Underground

1. Write your good qualities in the roots of the underground.

2. Include the results that your good qualities bring in the branches above ground.

the Underground

Changing Blame to Regret

Sad and angry feelings don't go away by themselves and can't be forced to go away. The worst thing someone could tell you is, "You shouldn't feel bad." Nothing could be further from the truth. You should feel bad.

The question is: Which kind of Bad?

1. I blame myself. or

2. I regret that I didn't do as well as I wanted to.

Blame is aggression.

Regret is disappointment.

Blame must be changed to Regret.

Success in holding the other person accountable depends on first clearing feelings of self-blame.

Repeat this exercise until you are OK accepting that you can't be perfect.

Don't pay attention to the scores. Momentary feelings cause the scores to change constantly.

> The Power of this exercise is the
> Daily Reminder, not the Daily Score.

I'm not blaming myself. I only feel regret.

0% true	25% true	50% true	75% true	100% true

I'm not blaming myself. I only feel regret.

0% true	25% true	50% true	75% true	100% true

I'm not blaming myself. I only feel regret.

0% true	25% true	50% true	75% true	100% true

AZURE FORTE

Realizing Inclusion

Not being included hurts.

Repair of the hurt begins with including oneself.

To become more included I talk about me instead of the other person. Example:

I don't say things like, "You forgot to call me!"

(This will cause a defensive reaction and I won't feel more included.)

Instead I say things like, "I was looking forward to getting your call. Did something happen?"

The examples on the right show the difference between self-inclusion and conflict.

FIELDING ANGER

Panel 1:
- "Let's stop at Sally's on the way to the party. I need to tell her about the new guy at work."
- "You always change our plans last minute. I'm sick of the way you complicate everything."

Panel 2:
- "Let's stop at Sally's on the way to the party. I need to tell her about the new guy at work."
- "I'd actually like to get to the party early so as not to miss the buffet."

An Exercise to Become More Included

Three Steps

1. Think of an incident of conflict with another person. Write down what you were trying to do. For example, "I was trying to have fun."

2. Now think about the other person's behavior. What might that other person have expected you to be doing? Example: "The other person was telling me all her troubles and she seemed to think it was my job to listen and give advice." Write down the job that the other person was giving you.

3. Using the drawing as you and another person. Say how you want to include yourself. Avoid statements with the word "you."

SUCCESS STORY

<u>Inclusion I Didn't Want</u>

Catherine and I met in a creative writing group. We had a lot in common, especially our passion for writing. Even though I come from a lower middle class working family and she from high-level wealth we had shared values and were completely comfortable with each other. It seemed like the cultural norms of our families were like foreign countries and we were like two adventurers in our own little world.

We bonded as friends and the closeness led to love and serious commitment. When we announced our intention to marry we were met with resistance from both our families. Catherine was not interested in a fancy lifestyle and we weren't worried that either of us would suffer cultural disagreement. We already had a shared life and laughed at her parents' insistence that we sign a pre-nuptial agreement. In order to earn the trust of my future in-laws I signed, but money issues were not a problem. Each of us worked with more interest in advancing our writing skills then in money. Catherine hated shopping and maintained casual dress. If we went out to eat we both preferred a late night diner as opposed to the fancy restaurant scene.

It was after one and a half years of marriage that another difficulty began. Catherine started traveling to writing seminars in Washington DC. Since we lived in New York City, which offers a wealth of study options, I found it puzzling. At first I thought nothing of it but the trips increased in frequency. Almost every other weekend she would leave and not return until the following Wednesday. Her work as an associate professor allowed her the flexible schedule while I had a Monday through Friday teaching week.

Eventually the truth came out. Catherine was involved with someone else, a woman. She talked about it tearfully, assuring me that she loved me and valued our marriage. She expressed a belief that she could not find a better husband but wanted to allow some time to understand herself. She did not want to lose me and did not want to give up her new relationship. While I expressed my intolerance of the affair I chose to wait it out, hoping she would return to our commitment.

I waited for another year and a half.

Along with the pain of rejection the issue of financial inequality showed up. Catherine had the means to do anything she wanted. She could have quit her job but she chose to teach. She could spontaneously purchase a last minute plane ticket and go anywhere she pleased and she did this frequently.

I wanted to also have the means to fly to another city and stay in a luxury hotel, to have some kind of distraction from the loneliness when she was away. Catherine would have covered this kind of expense for me but she knew that I would not tolerate the offer. I was already feeling like a groupie, waiting for her attention.

We both were agonized by the distortion of our relationship. For another half year I pressed Catherine to make a choice. Every time she considered giving up our marriage, or the other person, she cried and declared her love for me.

I tried countless methods of attempting to encourage Catherine to come to a decision. We went to marriage counseling and I picked up the "Realizing Inclusion" exercise. I've learned that this approach is actually a technique of sociometry called "Role Training or Role Theory." I saw the Role that I wanted Catherine to have - to make a choice and to choose me. Then I looked at the Role that Catherine had been expecting me to have. Clearly, I was supposed to just wait on the sidelines indefinitely. She did understand when I made my choice to refuse that role.

We each went our separate ways and wished each other well. I still marvel at the irony of thinking there was no difference between us. She didn't like to shop for clothes or furniture so I thought we were the same. It turned out that she was still privileged and accustomed to have anything she wanted.

At first she included me as a husband. Then I became a person waiting to be included as a husband. Then I became included with myself.

SUCCESS STORY

<u>Inclusion I Wanted</u>

I lived in the New England countryside with my two teenaged children. We had two cats, named Clover and Orange. The cats had a great country life, free to go out and return through the kitchen sliding screen door.

One day Orange brought a young stray cat home. I opened the door for Orange but did not let the other cat in, even though he was very cute. We were a two cat family and intended to stay that way. The young cat did not go away. He set up camp on the deck outside the screen door and left only to go off and return with Orange. After one and a half days he began to complain. He'd look at me through the screen and meow as if he was trying to tell me that he belonged to us. After a couple of days Orange hunted a chipmunk and put it down on the deck in front of the cat. Now it was even more clear that Orange had invited the cat to live with us.

I marveled at the endurance of the young cat's meowing. It was as if he already knew he would be living with us and waiting for me to realize the same. The tone of his voice was not annoying but almost a relentless effort to communicate. After four days I decided I would at least pick him up and pet him. He had no home and no people. But he clearly did have Orange who chose to remain neutral and let the matter get settled between the young cat and myself.

I stepped out onto the deck and picked him up. He began to purr and melted into my arms. In other words, I fell in love instantly. I had never had such a soft sweet feeling holding a cat so I named him Ambrose.

Approximately ten years later I suffered rejection. I was trying to become involved with a professional organization. While some participants were welcoming of me, there was strong resistance from numerous administrative members. It was horrible for me to not be completely accepted.

As I searched for resolution, I tried to understand the people who were rejecting me. I put myself in their shoes and tried to understand what they might feel. It was then that I remembered how I had rejected Ambrose at first, and even still Ambrose was sure that he belonged with us.

Role Reversing with the people who were rejecting me gave me my answer: I should be like Ambrose. From that point on I kept an Ambrose connection to the organization without the technique of complaining. Instead I just accepted the idea that some people had not yet understand that I belonged. Eventually they may or may not come to understand. Meanwhile I had my place and I entered into getting settled even though it wasn't perfect. Over time my inclusion became more and more warm and receptive. My level of comfort seemed to make others comfortable with me.

It's nice when inclusion is given by others automatically. But sometimes others need my help in understanding the wisdom of including me.

Dealing With A Bully

Knowing the Bully's Moves

Stopping aggression is like playing a mental game of chess. The advantage comes with understanding the Bully's moves.

The next exercises are teaching tools that reveal the mind of the bully and how to break up the abusive process.

FIELDING ANGER

1. Blue Shirt feels tense.

2. You're stupid

   Blue Shirt tries to get rid of tension by putting it onto Green Shirt.

3. Blue Shirt believes that the tension has been sent to Green Shirt.

67

SUCCESS STORY

I Learned His Moves and I Won

This is a pretty simple story. I was in a miserable situation: ordered to Anger Management by the Court and under supervision of the Department of Children and Families while they took custody of my kids. All of this had to do with my trying to fight back from my boyfriend's bullying.

We lived together in my apartment as a couple along with my children from a former marriage. He wasn't physically abusing me but driving me crazy in every other way. To make a long story short:

He managed to get control of the money and spent it on himself. We never had enough food.

He criticized me constantly and I argued back, trying to convince him and myself that I was a good person.

He was never around and I was always lonely.

He threatened to have my kids taken away whenever I got wound up and raised my voice.

He continually criticized my appearance and each time I felt more unattractive.

It was inevitable that a steady diet of the above would send me over the top and it did. One day I had a meltdown and lunged at him with my fists. That was his perfect opportunity to call the police.

The result was the required Anger Management Class and the temporary loss of custody of my kids. It was also my own wake up and the end of hoping he would change. I kicked him out and he had to go since he was now a trespasser.

Periodically he would show up unexpectedly to taunt me. You'd think I would refuse to see him but I was still afraid of him. He had called the police and got my kids taken away. Maybe he could make things even worse. The Anger Management class guided me towards building a strategy to replace my fear-based emotional outbursts.

The strategy was simple and reliable:

Don't let him see me get upset.

I discovered that I had a natural aptitude for "Knowing the Bully's Moves." It was so easy. He kept bullying me because he wanted to see me afraid, angry, and powerless.

All I had to do was not have the usual reactions to his emotional abuse. I let my anger work like a fuel line to power my strategic ability. It was wonderful to see him lose his confidence for controlling me.

I felt like I had won the lottery and my friends told me I was smiling like the Cheshire cat from Alice in Wonderland. The Department of Children and Families became satisfied with my new sense of calm and returned custody of my children to me.

The Mistake I Don't Want to Make

The story in the picture describes the most common mistake that keeps an argument going.

FIELDING ANGER

The argument keeps on going because G (Green Shirt) secretly worries that Bully's remark is true: "I'm stupid."

Avoiding a Trap

In the previous picture, "The Mistake I don't Want to Make," Green Shirt fell into a trap of worrying that the insult was true.

Logic has the hero's role in avoiding that trap.

Points of Logic to remember:

1. If I try to prove that I'm not stupid right now Bully won't be able to listen.

2. Bully wants to see me upset and defensive.

3. Abuse = accepting abusive remarks. End of Abuse = not accepting.

4. If I am truly inadequate, why would Bully need to tell me? It would already be obvious.

5. Bully is the one with the deep down feelings of being inadequate and is trying to throw them at me.

6. I'm not Bully's garbage can.

7. If I'm worried that I am inadequate I have to worry someplace else. I could be with a real helper, not with a bully.

SUCCESS STORY

<u>My Boss Was A Bully</u>

If you met Allison you'd encounter an elegant woman. Tall and beautiful she walked through the hallways of our rehab unit with her shoulders square, almost as though she was the lady of a manor instead of a senior officer. I was a regular counselor under her supervision in an Addiction Recovery Correctional Facility. The patients lived in residential units designed to build stability and success. One of their first steps of independence was to visit our building on their own without relapsing along the way. This wasn't easy since dealers in between the two locations could approach them.

I cared about the patients and gave my all to my work. Nevertheless I would only hear about what I was doing wrong in supervision with Allison. I knew, even before I went into our weekly meetings that I would be shown my submitted reports and told to correct minor errors such as, "Change "the" to "and the." Then she would talk about my progress notes and tell me what I should have done differently. I secretly called her "Lady Harpy." What about the good things I was doing? I never received affirmation or encouragement.

I was angry. In my own mind I thought she was messing up more as a supervisor than I was as a counselor. So what was going on for me in continually trying to gain her approval? Looking back on it I see the picture clearly. Without realizing it I was taking in the negativity. I had some good friends who would let me vent and call Allison a jerk and that felt good, but not good enough. I had a secret worry growing like a tumor, "Maybe I'm really not a very good counselor." Little by little I would end a work day feeling like a mediocre counselor at best. It grew to a strange feeling that crept over me during a session. It seemed like she was invisible, perched into the wall, watching me and deciding I was doing a poor job. Every once in a while I'd kind of role reverse with invisible Allison and see me. Was I doing a poor job or a good? I was unable to figure it out.

I was not doing a poor job - quite the opposite but Allison's psychological abuse left me in distress.

Then one day I overheard her talking to another senior officer about a difficult patient. Allison said, "I know exactly how to handle that guy. I had an abusive father and I've been there. I can set limits."

Given my level of misery I didn't feel the slightest guilt in ease dropping on this conversation. Tall confident statuesque Allison was an abuse victim. So that meant that the way she was treating me was the way she had been treated. (Perhaps a different version of abuse, but in the final analysis all abuse results in one person hurting another).

The accidental encounter triggered a turning point. I had previously seen Allison in a position I aspired to: "senior officer." Every supervision meeting had been clouded with my hidden longing, "Couldn't she offer her hand to help me reach higher ground? Why can't I belong?"

My new view saw Allison on level ground not higher ground. The unpleasant feeling in supervision meetings changed to an hour of sitting with a suffering person who needed to make someone else suffer.

It took a while for me to untangle my own underground emotional mess. The invisible Allison in the wall, watching me do a poor job, didn't go away instantly. It was gradual. A little bit of my own work with a counselor helped it fade faster. I've gotten pretty good at handling negativity, avoiding the mistake of letting secret worries sneak in if someone throws "pot shots" at me.

After all, people who are at peace with themselves don't project negative thoughts on others.

Victimization happens, no matter how hard I try to avoid it.

Exploring All Options

- My computer gets hacked.

- People cut in front of me at the check out line.

- Co-workers give me a hard time.

- Advertisements include lies about the product.

- Even when I do my best I will still sometimes fall victim.

What are my options?

Worst Option:

I can think of myself as a victim.

Best Option:

I can think of myself as a strong person who was victimized.

Avoiding the Land of the Lost

The Land of the Lost is not a geographic place. It is a style of living. In 1968 Steven Karpman wrote an excellent description of the lost life style called "The Victim Rescuer Persecutor Triangle." The application of Karpman's triangle has become widespread.

Beliefs that get people lost:

- Being a victim is your true identity.

- You will feel better if you rescue someone, despite the rescue being unnecessary.

- Hurting someone, or yourself, will solve a problem.

Real Victim vs Lost Victim

A person who does not have the Victim Identity manages to stay out of the Land of the Lost, "I'm a smart and capable person who sometimes gets victimized. When that happens I find a way to get over the bad experience."

The Victim Identity

A Bully is a person who tries to convince other people that they are victims. A person who accepts the Bully's effort has the Victim Identity, "Poor me. I'm always getting bullied and there isn't anything I can do about it. It's like I'm wearing a sign that says 'It's OK to hurt me.' Why do more bad things happen to me than to other people?"

```
        Victim
         /\
        /  \
       /    \
      /      \
     /        \
    /_____\
Rescuer       Persecutor
```

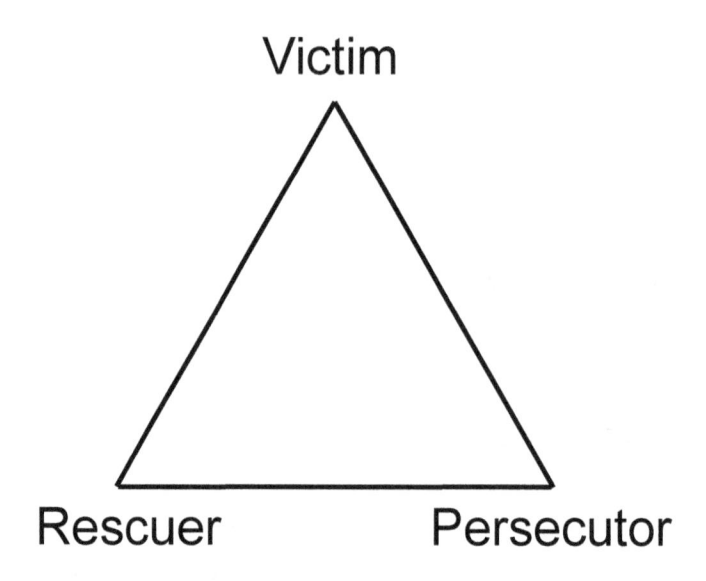

If you are any one of these you will automatically be the other two.

Rescuer: also a victim and a persecutor
Persecutor: also a rescuer and a victim.
Victim: also a persecutor and a rescuer

Victim, Persecutor, Rescuer
How does this rotation happen?

The victim in this triangle is actually a lost victim, not a real victim needing a real rescue. A person caught in the triangle trap continually asks for help unnecessarily without trying to build inward strength. Example:

Victim
Mary drives a rundown, poorly maintained car. She doesn't stop to realize that her income would allow her to buy and maintain a reliable car. She regularly calls her friends to rescue her when her car breaks down on the way to shopping or work.

Persecutor
Because Mary does not seek a solution to her car dilemma and repeatedly expects her friends to drop what they are doing to come to her rescue she is abusing their time and energy.

Rescuer
Mary is unaware of her choices and feels victimized by life. She has a friend who feels the same way. That friend expects Mary to engage in long late night phone conversations. As Mary listens to her friend she grows tired and desires sleep. Nevertheless she is compelled to stay on the phone fighting sleep and giving the kind of rescue that she, herself, desires.

(For another example see the next success story, Help! Help?)

The Lost Rescuer Identity

A real rescue person joins rescue teams to save people caught in an avalanche or trapped in a burning building. These victims truly can't help themselves.

A Lost Rescuer doesn't realize when the rescue is not needed. It takes skill and practice to know the difference. The role of the Lost Rescuer is a common lure into the victim, rescuer, persecutor triangle.

Lost rescuing can hurt.

SUCCESS STORY

HELP! HELP?

Gloria was living in a home for the disabled. She was discharged with no explanation. Previous to that home she had been living with her adult daughter and eleven-year-old granddaughter, but the daughter also sent her away. We thought the rift between them was stress-related due to the daughter's unplanned pregnancy.

The night that Gloria came to our recovery meeting stating that she would be homeless in a few days some of us got together to help. We've been a pretty tight group for years and we give our recovery work credit for success. Gloria had been with us for several months and we found her to be sweet and good-natured. The thought of seeing her in a homeless shelter was intolerable so we talked it over to figure out options.

I knew a guy who ran a boarding house. Getting her linked up was going to be a problem as she wasn't assertive and would have chosen the homeless shelter over meeting someone new and asking for a room. I was the only one who could take an afternoon off from work to go with her to meet the guy and see the place. It worked out. He accepted her as a tenant and I felt that trading the afternoon's pay was worthwhile.

The following Saturday the guys got together and moved Gloria's stuff to her new place. The owner let her have a space in the common room for a piece of furniture she didn't want to part with. The following Tuesday we had a celebration for her at our meeting.

Four months went by. New England winter melted into spring and we saw Gloria on and off. Then one Tuesday she came to our meeting and shared another sad story: once again she was being asked to leave her residence.

We just couldn't figure this out. Gloria was like a little sister who never made waves, always expressing a worry about being intrusive. How could she possibly have caused a problem at her new residence? I gave the boarding house guy a call but he refused to talk about it.

Again Gloria talked about going to the shelter. The guys who had previously lived there were worried about her safety. Again we tried to help.

Someone from our group had been receiving services from a Christian Charity and suggested that Gloria apply. Because she had previously been a resident in a home for the disabled she was given serious consideration. We didn't know what her disability was but were only interested in helping her.

I was glad to give her a ride to the charity office. That day she had just returned from a train trip to New York City and was acting kind of feisty. Her grandchild had been born a month ago and her daughter had moved to New York with the children to live with a new boyfriend. The daughter was still rejecting her so Gloria chose to surprise them and just show up.

The next day a nagging feeling crept over me about the whole conversation. If Gloria was too anxious to meet a potential new landlord, how could she grab a train to New York City on her own and then show up on her daughter who didn't want to see her? Something was wrong with this picture. At the next Tuesday meeting a group member reported that Gloria had discharged herself from the Christian Service because she didn't like their temporary emergency housing. She never came back to our meeting.

The whole saga left me feeling used. It's like she was yelling, "Help! I'm drowning," and we all steered our boats off course to go to her. Then when we threw her a life preserver she said, "I didn't want a pink life preserver. I wanted a blue one."

I still like to help but am trying to know when to help and how much to give. The Gloria Saga was a clear example of the VRP triangle.

Victim: Gloria came to us acting helpless and powerless.

Rescuer: We tried to rescue her but she wasn't helping herself.

Persecutor: Gloria didn't have a problem in using our time, money and energy. Even if she didn't realize what she was doing and we didn't see what we were walking into, we were getting hurt.

When Rescue Hurts the Person You Try to Help

You hurt the person you are trying to rescue when:

1. The person being rescued isn't really helpless. The continuing rescue makes the person feel more helpless.

2. The person being rescued has gained confidence in the rescuer but has lost self-confidence.

3. The person being rescued develops a belief that a rescuer must always be found.

4. The job of solving the problem gets taken away from the person being rescued.

When Rescue Hurts Yourself

You hurt yourself when:

1. No matter how hard you try the person asking for help does not feel better and continues to ask for more. This makes the rescuer a victim.

2. You become the person who is always "the only one who can make things OK" and wind up constantly putting your own life on hold. You are included with others as a human safety net but when you want to be involved in your own life you are less popular.

3. You feel another person's pain and without realizing you are trying to make it stop for yourself, more than for the other person. "I'll feel better when I'm not feeling your pain, so I'll take care of it for you."

Aggression is a verbal, physical or indirect attack.

Stopping the Cycle of Aggression

Aggression becomes a cycle when the victimized person gets mad and counter attacks. Then the person who was first aggressive gets mad about being the target of the counter attack and attacks back, on and on.

When the Cycle of Aggression starts each person becomes victim and perpetrator combined.

Each person caught in the Cycle believes that the way to stop the aggression is to win. This doesn't work because the loser tries to find a new chance to win and starts the whole thing all over again.

> In a Cycle of Aggression both participants have the option to be aggressors as well as victims. This is very different from violent attacks against helpless victims.

> Even though the perpetrator started the aggression, it is the victim who has the chance to stop the Cycle.

Stopping aggression is like playing a mental game of chess. The advantage comes when the victim understands the Perpetrator's moves.

Perpetrator's First Move: Trying to release tension by throwing anger onto the victim.

Victim's Successful Next Move: The Victim does not accept the attack.

Check Mate – Game Over: The Perpetrator loses the chance to throw anger onto the Victim.

FIELDING ANGER

Blue Shirt wants to get rid of tension.

Blue Shirt tries to feel better by making Green Shirt a target for tension, but Green Shirt won't be a target

"You're Stupid"

"My choice is to not get involved"

"I actually don't see myself as stupid."

Now Blue Shirt feels worse than before.

Blue Shirt Will Try Again . . . and again, and again, and again.

The Final Move In The Move that Works

Each time there will be more anger and it will be more difficult to choose not getting involved. But getting back at Blue Shirt will make the cycle of aggression last longer.

Without a counter attack from Green Shirt, Blue Shirt will get more and more tired with each try.

The final move will be Green Shirt's final success in not getting involved. Blue Shirt will give up and the cycle of aggression will be broken.

Unfortunately the conflict that Blue Shirt feels on the inside will remain strong. Blue Shirt will look for someone else to involve in continued conflict.

SUCCESS STORY

Going It Alone Is Not The Answer

"I come from a family that believes in violence. It's like I was raised to learn aggression with my mother's milk. The men in my family have been to jail and are proud of the violence they learned there.

I don't want that life but it's hard to turn away from the surroundings you grew up with. The angry feelings come so easily and the urge to be aggressive scares me.

I work in a food service warehouse doing heavy lifting, loading and packing. The nature of the job puts me in the company of men who follow the old macho way to be. I don't want to talk about fights I've won, or superiority over women. When I don't join in the aggression talk I see them look at each other with sarcastic expressions. To make it worse I'm the only black guy on some of the shifts and I get remarks thrown at me about my race. Then I go on break and someone makes a sarcastic comment on how good I'll feel when I have a better job, trying to insinuate that I can't get a better job.

I go to trade school at night to become a computer technician. I hope I will someday work with people who are friendly and considerate. But now I'm alone and afraid that I won't be able to hold back my anger at work. I don't want to wind up in jail like the other men in my family.

"The Final Move in the Move That Works" makes sense. It means that you just don't play when someone is throwing anger at you. This is so hard to do. I can't help but feel insecure and worried that I really am a looser some of the time. My feelings to strike back are like a magnet pulling at me to lunge at someone. If I did I would get fired and have no income.

At school I heard about a support group for anger problems. The first meeting was last night and I went to it. Only five people were there, some of them ordered by the court or on probation. Still, the climate wasn't like my family or day job. Nobody was talking tough and we even joked and shared some stories. If I'm going to succeed in using the Move That Works I need to be with other people who want the same thing. Going it alone is not the answer, and it's not *the tough show of strength it pretends to be. I can have hope if I choose people who want to be with me, not people who want to fight with me."*

The Land of the Future

The Land of the Future is not a geographic place. It is a lifestyle that works for today.

Living in the land of the Future requires 21st Century Anger, not Cave Man Anger. There is a big difference.

> 21st Century Anger uses the skill of thinking before you act, even though you don't want to.

FIELDING ANGER

1. "You're Stupid"

   Green Shirt feels victimized by Blue Shirt.

2. feelings ◯ logic

   Green Shirt takes time.

3. How angry am I at Blue Shirt?
   How angry am I at Me?

   Green Shirt explores feelings and facts.

SUCCESS STORY

I Chose The Future

> There is a difference between a bully and a person who acts with aggression by mistake.

There are many places where art therapists are treated like "air head zany artists." I managed to get a job where I felt respected, offering art therapy at a psychiatric crisis center.

The Executive Director, Rick, was a mild mannered psychologist. The Assistant Director, Ed, just finishing his Ph.D. in Psychology, was pleasant and enthusiastic. They made a good team. Then Rick accepted a new position away from city life.

It's amazing how the person at the top can set the tone for everyone else. As soon as Rick announced his plan to leave, Ed's behavior changed. If we asked Ed a question it turned out to be a marathon of listening to him expound on his knowledge. He was tense. Consults with him felt tense.

We had a send off dinner for Rick, expressing our gratitude and regret in losing him. Ed became the new director. A social worker, Julie, was also brought on board to serve as immediate supervisor of the in-patient unit where I worked. She was new to us but we truly loved the way she managed her responsibilities. I was happy when I was promoted to the title of "Senior Clinician," and it was my job to take over for her if she was absent.

Working at crisis services felt like Camelot until Julie announced that she was moving out of state. We gave her a beautiful heartfelt goodbye and Ed orchestrated the search for Julie's replacement.

During the four month hiring interim the in-patient unit continued to function smoothly. It was clear that my abilities as temporary unit supervisor were strong. During one of our weekly staff meetings I received a round of applause from counselors and administrators alike. I felt validated and ready to make an official application for the position.

On several occasions Ed told me I was not a strong candidate and explained why, "We need the coordination of a trained social worker who uses the language of professional psychiatric consultation. You don't know this language and the professional staff here has difficulty understanding you. If you want to learn it will take a long time but you could set that as a goal."

I don't know why I didn't just ditch my application right then and there, but I decided to follow through with what I had started. A full hiring committee was in place but Ed did not include the committee when it was time to make a choice. He put someone he chose independently into the position, ironically a social worker who had been fired from her previous position.

I was hopeful that I would get along with Stacy, the new supervisor, but she was judgmental and critical towards me. One day she saw me in my daily routine of placing my purse in the locked drawer of my desk and she said, "I don't like the idea of your locking your purse up like that. It makes you look paranoid." Since every care provider in the building who had a purse routinely locked it into a desk drawer I did not engage with her on this theme. She had a daily arsenal of attacking things to say, leaving no space available for dialogue.

She made negative reports about me to Ed. Then he would speak with me about her accusations and not accept my explanations. He said, "There is a difference between a social worker who is a supervisor and an art therapist under her supervision. I can only believe one of you and I choose to believe the social worker."

I accepted a new position with another outpatient therapy clinic nearby. Many of our patients were also enrolled there and I already had a good rapport with some of the professional staff. One of the administrators welcomed me with complimentary statements about my work in crisis service. I felt better already.

Ed suggested that we have an "exit interview" and I was not into arguing with him about anything so I attended. Perhaps my leaving opened the door for a tension-free meeting. Ed surprised me with an affirmation, albeit a strange one. "You scare me," he said. "I see very disturbed patients come in here quite ill and work with you. Then I see them go out well. It's scary to see that happen in such a short time frame."

Then he asked me to offer my "exit interview" remarks about the operation of the crisis center. I thought about it and decided not to try defending myself from the unfair events that had occurred. Instead I just gave him eye contact and said, "Ed, I only hope that you will some day realize that you've made a mistake."

When I went to my new job I felt insecure in making case presentations to psychiatrists because I had been told by Ed that I lacked clarity.

I would apologize about my wording and would restructure my sentences in an attempt to be understood. Finally one of them asked me about it. I explained that I had been told that my presentations aren't professional, that colleagues have a hard time understanding me. The psychiatrist then informed me that my presentations were quite clear and professional and she had no difficulty understanding me at all.

From that moment on I had complete confidence in my ability to use professional language. I realized that the language clarity criticism was another example of "The Mistake I Don't Want to Make" - my worry that the negative things said about me were really true.

I wish that Ed knew how valuable my exit interview had been and that I feel only good when I think about him. His negative opinion about my professional language seemed like a small irritation in comparison to the generous affirmation he gave me. I've never since been employed under a director who would disclose the level of honest feelings that Ed had in the exit interview. Ed was sincere. Perhaps he understood my art therapist's view of his mistake as a validation. In my own identity I'm included as a person who makes mistakes. In an artist's way of life mistakes can't be avoided, so we may as well make friendly use of them.

I was launched forward in my new position with more self-assurance than I had ever had before. After all, I had already been applauded by the greater community for my work as a temporary supervisor and had enjoyed day-to-day success in that job. The question of my use of professional language was settled rather quickly and my understanding of my ability to help people was greatly endorsed by Ed. Nothing stood in the way of my continued professional growth.

A few years later I learned that Ed's new social worker, Stacy, only lasted one year in that job. I went on to becoming a Senior Supervising Clinician in a nearby agency.

> It is human to have impulsive instincts.
>
> It is also human to learn new skills.
>
> New skills become new instincts.

How to Learn a New Skill

1. Forget about getting it right all the time. (Let's face it: James Bond is a character of fiction. Regular human beings can't be that good at winning all the time.)

2. At first you will only get it right 1 out of every 10 tries (more or less). Keep practicing.

3. Repeatedly trying will grow the number of times you succeed. Soon you will succeed 2 times out of 10. Then 3 out of 10, then 4 & 5 out of 10.

4. You will find yourself automatically using the new skill. It may or may not take time. Your desire to have the new skill is your guarantee to achieve it.

21st Century Skills

Many human instincts tell us to do things that won't work. New Skills are needed.

Human Instinct: telling someone off.

Needed Skill: before telling someone off, automatically understanding that the other person won't listen.

Human Instinct: to blame.

Needed Skill: to understand that

1. blame is a form of aggression and creates more conflict.

2. it's never all one person's fault.

3. "accountability" can be requested without conflict.

Human Instinct: to worry excessively about making mistakes.

Needed Skill: to understand that mistakes guide the path to success.

Human Instinct: thinking that "followers and leaders" make the world go round.

Needed Skill: to find the "good team players and leaders" who make the world go round. Become a good team player and a good leader.

Human Instinct: to forget that it is human to have self-blame.

Needed Skill: to automatically nurture self acceptance.

Human Instinct: to tell a friend or partner how to be a better friend.

Needed Skill: to tell a friend or partner more about yourself, the ways of being together that make you feel good and those that make you feel bad.

12 Tips for Resolving a Conflict With Another Person

1. Make sure that your spoken words, mood and tone are not harsh or attacking.

2. Will the other person listen even if your approach is respectful? If the other person can't listen, even when you are offering respect, stop your effort and don't continue to try.

3. Listen well to the other person.

4. Don't accept judgmental or attacking remarks. If one is made say, "I don't accept attacking remarks" or "I can't hear what you are saying because I feel blamed."

5. Role reverse with the other person: Put yourself in the other person's place. Try to see and feel through the other's eyes and heart. This will allow for much more understanding.

6. Avoid making peace by offering to take blame. Don't say, "It's my fault."

7. Avoid blame. Don't say, "It's your fault."

8. Talk about the conflict as though it were a 3rd person involved or a situation that you both found yourselves in. Say things like, "This happened because I thought you were saying something else."

9. An apology leads to more difficulty if it is given simply to end the conflict and not because you feel genuine regret.

10. An apology only works if it is offered without self blame and includes self respect.

11. Ask for what you need. Some examples:

    - Can we continue to talk with each other again until we have gotten things straightened out?

    - Can we meet in person instead of by telephone?

    - Would you be willing to remind me if you see me starting to do the thing that bothered you?

12. Suggest co-creating a plan to avoid the same disagreement to happen again.

"Who Shall Survive?"

"Who Shall Survive" is the title of a book written by Dr. Jacob Levy Moreno. The first edition was published in 1934.

The title describes the book's purpose, offered in the form of a question: What discoveries can we make to allow for the survival of humankind? To approach this task Dr. Moreno founded the field of Sociometry; "Sociometry deals with all the two-way relationships between individuals."

Survival skills are learned through relationships with others and with self. We will survive if we learn to create healthy relationships instead of attacking each other. Holding onto self-attacking behavior also prevents success.

This Field Guide gives a lot of attention to self-acceptance which is often forgotten within the confusion of conflict.

Sociometry

The main job of a Sociometrist is to help create a healthy world that includes everyone. Sociometric skills help us co-create a healthy world together:

- Building healthy interpersonal relationships and communities

- Creative thinking and teamwork

- Seeing and understanding all points of view without cruel criticism

- Honoring Inclusion; Avoiding Isolation

- Adjusting to change with spontaneity

- Using and creating scientific charts, measurements and diagrams

- Discovering new solutions to old problems.

Sociometric methods are used in the health professions, education, business, law enforcement, the military, and many more.

Reader's Guide

How Tools Get Used: A Walk Through

The final story, "I Chose the Future" includes the use of most skills from the Tool Box. If a skill wasn't used there is a good reason why. The following notes outline how each tool was used or not needed by the person who shared her story. We'll call her "Annie."

1. **What Causes Anger?**
   Annie's anger was triggered because of feeling repressed, attacked, not being included, treated with indifference and judged.

2. **Putting Brain Power Up Front and Letting Logic In**
   Annie did not counter-attack Stacy's bullying, not once. Instead of following her feelings impulsively she stopped to think about what to do.

3. **Fact and Feeling Team Work**
   Annie felt angry, sad and not fairly treated as a candidate, but she remembered being given a round of applause for her work as a supervisor. She accepted her feelings and combined them with facts to determine if she was truly unqualified.

4. **Six Step Work Sheet**
   Annie was not involved in counter-attacking Stacy or Ed and therefore did not have to work through the six steps. She did allow herself the possibility of lacking professional language skills and did not get angry at herself because of it.

5. **The Double Down Dilemma**
   There could be times when it is wise to prove oneself,

but in this case Annie knew it would accomplish nothing. Annie didn't have a hidden bad feeling about herself and didn't want to waste her time pondering over her bad feelings about Ed and Stacy's behavior. Instead she tried to decide on a next step. This was a way of moving towards her future rather than staying stuck in a painful present.

6. **Exploring the Underground**
   Unseen feelings are typically the cause for attacking aggressive behavior. Annie's anger was not hidden. Her stronger feeling was a desire to avoid a cycle of conflict and to move her life forward.

7. **Changing Blame to Regret**
   Annie did not spend a lot of time trying to blame Stacy, Ed or herself. This would have been a waste of time. Blame doesn't work. She never did find out if Ed saw himself as having made a mistake. Nevertheless she looked at the positive results of the affirmation he gave her and validated human error as a part of life.

8. **Realizing Inclusion**
   Annie could have been included with Stacy if she accepted Stacy's aggression. Inclusion with Ed would require Annie to accept not being believed when she tried to tell him her experience. She would have to accept his judgment of her as unqualified for a leadership role that she was already performing well. She chose not to include herself with those conditions. When she could not achieve inclusion for her true self she moved forward to having authentic inclusion in a new place.

9. **Dealing with a Bully and Knowing the Bully's Moves**
Stacy had the behavior of a bully. Ed did not. His idea that Annie was not qualified seemed to be something that he believed, rather than an attempt to attack Annie. He criticized her professional language skills but he did not criticize her job performance as a temporary unit supervisor. He was honest in affirming her clinical skills with patients and shared his own feelings of vulnerability in the exit interview. Stacy never offered affirmation to Annie and made attacking criticisms that were not even logical.

10. **Knowing the Bully's Moves**
It did not take long for Annie to figure out Stacy's moves. Stacy was seeking to have complete control over Annie and to reduce Annie's level of self-confidence. In observing Stacy's behavior Annie chose not to try to convince Stacy to see her in a positive light. She saw that Stacy did not choose to listen. Annie was always one step ahead of Stacy.

11. **The Mistake I Don't Want To Make**
Annie didn't secretly worry about Stacy's criticisms. She saw them for what they were, attempts at aggression. Annie did worry about Ed's negative opinion of her professional language skills. Rather than letting worry overtake her she attempted to address this possible area of weakness when she moved on to her new job. There she learned that her worry was a mistake. Annie did not fear or bury mistakes. Instead she thought of them as a natural part of life.

12. **Avoiding A Trap**
Annie did not get trapped into conflict. She saw that she was dealing with a bully and she moved out of the way every time an attacking event occurred.

13. Avoiding The Land of The Lost

The Land of the Lost is a slang expression for being stuck in the Victim, Persecutor, Lost Rescuer Triangle. Annie would have been pulled in if she had behaved like a drowning victim, hoping someone would save her from her dilemma. Instead she took pro-active measures to find a solution and remained captain of her own ship in her quest.

14. Stopping The Cycle of Aggression

The cycle of aggression begins when the person being attacked makes a counter-attack. Annie was attacked repeatedly by Stacy but Annie knew better than to participate in conflict. Ed seemed unaware that his behavior was passive aggressive:

1. Trying to convince Annie that it would take a long time for her to build professional language skills, and

2. Telling Annie that other colleagues had a hard time understanding her, but giving no examples of times that the lack of understanding occurred.

In both of the above Ed tried to convince Annie that she had fewer choices in building her future.

Logic draws the conclusion that Ed was convinced that Annie lacked language skills and was unaware of his aggression, a common human experience.

15. The Move That Works

Annie chose to not get involved with Stacy's obvious attempt to create conflict. With Ed it was not obvious but

Annie recognized that Ed was not offering a level conversation with her to discuss his reservations about her qualifications. Telling Annie that other people held a negative opinion of her abilities left her choosing to be cautious. She had not heard this directly from her coworkers and did not try to defend herself. Defensive behavior is a type of counter-attack and keeps an aggressive cycle going.

Instead Annie stepped aside by telling Ed, "I hope that someday you will realize that you've made a mistake." This was her way of saying, "This matter now completely belongs to you and I don't have a part in it."

Tool Reference Guide

This reference guide helps find a place to start when searching for solutions. Opening the book to the middle can work fine as long as " The Most Important Things to Know," have been reviewed.

Tools That Can Help When . . . .

I'm told that I shouldn't be angry:
  Changing Blame to Regret, page 52
  Exercise to Become More Included, page 57

I want to be aggressive, to "fight fire with fire":
  Letting Logic Have a Say, page 28
  21st Century Skills, page 108

I want to keep the peace by 'just letting go of my anger ':
  Four Types of Aggression, page 16
  Six-Step Anger Event Worksheet, page 34

I'm down and out from being victimized:
  Avoiding the Land of the Lost, page 79

I feel guilty:
  Blaming and Judging in The Most Important Things to Know, page 13
  The Double-down Dilemma, page 44
  Exploring the Underground, page 47
  Changing Blame to Regret, page 54

I want to get even:
  What Doesn't Work and What Works, page 17
  Stopping the Cycle of Aggression, page 90–95

I want to fight for fairness:
    21st Century Skills, page 108–110
    Letting Logic Have a Say, page 28
    What Doesn't Work and What Works, page 17

I'm being blamed, even though I'm not to blame:
    Realizing Inclusion, page 55–59

Trying to work it out isn't working:
    Stopping the Cycle of Aggression, page 90–95
    12 Tips for Resolving a Conflict With Another Person, page 111
    Going it Alone is Not the Answer, page 98

I don't know why I feel angry:
    What Causes Anger? page 20
    Six Step Anger Event Worksheet, page 34
    Realizing Inclusion, page 55–59

I'm angry and I don't know what to do about it:
    Letting Logic Have a Say, page 28
    Fact and Feeling Team Work, page 30
    Six Step Anger Event Work Sheet, page 34

I'm angry and I don't want to be angry:
    Anger is a Personal Feeling, page 12
    What Causes Anger, page 20
    Realizing Inclusion, page 55–59
    21st Century Skills, page 108
    12 Tips for Resolving a Conflict With Another Person, page 111
    How to Learn a New Skill, page 107

Discussion Group Guidelines

More than 5 people in a discussion group are probably too many. A larger group can be broken into 2 or 3 small groups.

Choose the Discussion Topic:

At the beginning of each meeting make a group decision. Avoid using the whole discussion time to decide.

or

Start at page 1 and gradually discuss each page as meetings continue. This will allow maximum time for discussion.

Achieve a group agreement on discussion rules. Include the following:

Confidentiality
Personal disclosures within the group may not be repeated outside the group. Conversations between group members outside the meetings can only focus on those present. Group members who are not present may not be discussed.

Shared Space
Each group member will have a chance to contribute. If a group member tends to take too much time, other group members will explain their own needs to have adequate time to share and will not blame or criticize the person who takes too much time.

Understand Quiet Group Members
If a group member makes very few contributions other group members will express interest in what the quiet person is thinking and accept the person's choice to share or mostly listen.

Finish On Time
Honor the time to conclude. Some group members are not able to stay late.

It takes a long time to create a healthy self.

J.L. Moreno

Acknowledgments

Deep appreciation is given to Donna Little, whose guidance has been a chamber in the heart of this project.

My son, Zack whose suggestions were made from an in-depth understanding of our culture and a keen awareness.

My daughter, Zoe, who gave strong endorsement and set many examples of how to be.

Ann Hale, whose guidance has helped me see this project and see myself.

Zerka T. Moreno for noticing me at unlikely times and guiding me from the periphery to a centered place.

All those who have worked with tools of Fielding Anger. Each contribution is a continuing creative hand.

J.L. Moreno, wherever he may be.

Afterward

This book was created from the work of action, exploration and experience. The tools and exercises have been practiced within real life interactions of individuals. Highly educated professionals and, in contrast, adults who did not complete high school stepped forward to apply the tools at home or work and report on the results. Each individual's professional position did not have any bearing on the potential for success. Those deprived of formal education, but not deprived of intelligence and spontaneity, fostered some of the most perceptive learning.

The field of Sociometry began with J.L. Moreno. His biography in its wonder and suspense was written by René Marineau, published in 1989 by Tavistock/Routledge; *Jacob Levy Moreno 1889–1974*.

In 2012 Zerka T. Moreno completed her lifetime memoirs, edited by Edward Schreiber, published by Mental Health Resources; *To Dream Again, A Memoir*. Her personal accounts of life and work in a pioneering partnership with Dr. Moreno affords the reader enough intrigue to supersede a Harry Potter volume.

The biographies by Marineau and Zerka are graceful and informative introductory readings. They feed the imagination and form a literary tidal estuary from which flows an ocean of resources and supports.

If a good read is the reader's desire John Nolte's *The Philosophy, Theory and Methods of J. L. Moreno: The Man Who Tried to Become God*, is the book of choice. Published by Routledge in 2015. The intrigue that the subtitle suggests, "The Man Who Tried to Become God," turns out to reveal the underside of the statement: Moreno's quest to support man in becoming man / woman becoming woman / society reaching its potential to become itself. It will be difficult to surpass this book, which offers pleasure in reading and clear insight of Moreno's offering.

A reprint of Moreno's biography is now available on the website of the American Society of Group Psychotherapy and Psychodrama (ASGPP). Who Shall Survive is now a rare book but a modern age one, also available on the website.

The discovery of support is an individual journey, best navigated by logic and propelled by sails filled with the breath of spontaneous adventure.